Original title:
Ocean Dreams in the Tropics

Copyright © 2025 Creative Arts Management OÜ
All rights reserved.

Author: Jameson Hartfield
ISBN HARDBACK: 978-1-80581-650-8
ISBN PAPERBACK: 978-1-80581-177-0
ISBN EBOOK: 978-1-80581-650-8

Whispers of the Cerulean Tide

Flip-flops dance on sand so bright,
Seagulls squawk in sheer delight.
A sunburned crab with tiny claws,
Escapes the waves without a pause.

Turtles wearing hats so blue,
Wave hello to passing crew.
The fish all giggle, swim and glide,
As beach balls float like ocean pride.

Sunlit Shores and Floating Hopes

A beach ball bounces off my head,
Landing near the seagull's spread!
Sandcastles built, then washed away,
Like dreams that drift in sunny play.

Sandy toes and giggles roar,
As sunscreen flies, I beg for more.
Umbrellas tipping, drinks would spill,
While laughter echoes, time stands still.

Beneath the Coconut Canopy

Coconuts falling with a thud,
While sipping juice, I made a mud!
A monkey grins, a cheeky tease,
As I chase him, giggling with ease.

Banana boats that sail with flair,
Twirly pirouettes fill the air.
Flipping fish just want to bite,
As I dance under the moonlight.

A Symphony of Salt and Serenity

Waves that crash like clumsy cows,
Remind me not to take a bow.
Salty snacks and goofy dives,
A splash attack, oh how it thrives!

With each wave, a joke unfurls,
Mermaids throw their pranks and twirls.
A floating hat, a lost flip-flop,
In this carnival, we laugh non-stop.

Breathing in the Warmth of Waves

Sunshine tickles sandy toes,
Seagulls squawk in funny prose.
A crab in shades, it struts with flair,
Chasing flip-flops, unaware of where.

Waves come crashing, what a sight,
Splashing humans, laughter in flight.
A dolphin leaps, it does a dance,
While tourists try their best to prance.

The Interlude of Restless Waters

A coconut rides on a playful swell,
It spins and spins, oh what a yell!
Kids are diving, making a splash,
While adults sip drinks and just bask.

A fish in sunglasses swims on by,
Rooting for swimmers to try and fly.
Tides oblivious to our grand plans,
They just giggle, tickle our tans.

Horizons Blended in Twilight Hues

Sunsets paint with wild delight,
A flamingo in swirls takes flight.
Beach chairs tumble in the breeze,
As laughter echoes through the trees.

A sunset toast, what do we cheer?
To the seaweed tangled in our beer!
Stars peek out, all dressed to shine,
As we mix cocktails with a splash of brine.

Chords of the Undulating Surf

Waves play music, a funny tune,
Shells tap dance beneath the moon.
Sandy toes and giggles swell,
As jellyfish perform their spell.

A starfish strums on a seaweed guitar,
While clams cheer from their sandbar.
Bubbles rise in a frothy cheer,
As everyone laughs, 'We want more beer!'

Secrets in the Surf

Waves crash like laughter, so bright,
A crab in shorts gives quite a fright.
Sandcastles tumble, what a sight,
Seagulls compete in a silly flight.

Turtles on surfboards, take a spin,
While fish throw parties, where to begin?
The jellyfish tango, a funny grin,
In this wacky world, we all fit in.

Mosaic of Tidal Whispers

Shells gossip softly, secrets they share,
A dolphin dresses in bright underwear.
Starfish sell jokes, with flair and care,
While the seaweed dances with wild hair.

Octopuses juggle, eyes all around,
The crabs play poker on the sandy ground.
With every wave, laughter is found,
In this quirky realm, joy abounds.

A Horizon Bathed in Gold

Sunrise in shades of bubblegum hues,
The lobsters wear glasses, sporting blue shoes.
A pelican struts, talent to choose,
While the tide tells tales of colorful clues.

Mermaids giggle, tails in a tangle,
They've mastered the art of silly wrangle.
The sand is a blanket where dreams dangle,
As the sun dips low, and friendships wrangle.

Parakeets and Moonbeams

Parakeets sing off-key, not so sweet,
While crickets are grooving to a funky beat.
The moon winks, dressed in silvery sheet,
And the stars join in for a late-night treat.

Frogs throw a dance that's out of sight,
With flashlights in hand, they twirl in delight.
A clam crafts a crown, looking just right,
Under the glow of the moon's gentle light.

Sails of Distant Horizons

On wobbly boards, we set to sail,
With snacks in hand and one big whale.
The captain's hat is far too tight,
He can't see straight, but what a sight!

A parrot squawks, with feathered glee,
It's stealing chips right off of me.
The wind's a giggle, the waves a cheer,
We laugh till dawn, not a single fear.

Lullabies of the Sandy Shore

A crab did tap dance with great flair,
While sunburned tourists squinted, 'Where?'
A flip-flop flies, it's all the rage,
As sand clings tight, we're in a cage.

We build a castle, not so grand,
Two towers, moats, and a seashell band.
A seagull swoops, he steals our lunch,
Peace out, crab, it's time to crunch!

Embrace of the Aqua Breeze

The breeze whispers sweet, or maybe it shouts,
While sun hats sail like boats in bouts.
A jellyfish winks, "Come dance with me!"
I'm stuck to the shore - nope, not for me.

With sunscreen smeared in a goofy way,
We laugh it off, come join the play.
The tide rolls in, brings seaweed hair,
Come join the fun if you've got a spare!

A Dance of Sunlit Waves

The sunflowers dance with the ocean breeze,
They grab a drink, but spill it with ease.
Turtles do backflips, oh what a show,
While we sit and munch on nachos, you know?

The beach ball bounces, a hit or a miss,
We dive for it, no chance for bliss.
With giggles and splashes, we race with glee,
Each wave a giggle, come swim with me!

The Call of the Swaying Palm

The palm tree wiggles, quite a sight,
Dancing to the rhythm, oh what delight.
It calls to the coconuts, 'Come on, let's sway!'
While I try to catch them, they roll away!

The beach is a party, shells spin on the sand,
Crabs having a disco, isn't it grand?
Seagulls are swooping, practicing dives,
While I take a tumble, but hey, I survive!

Drift Into the Horizon's Embrace

On a floaty banana, I'm sailing with flair,
Waving at dolphins who play without care.
The sun's overly friendly, got too much cheer,
A two-tone lobster hops, "Hey, join me here!"

With waves giving high-fives, I smile and grin,
A fish in a tuxedo just slid right in.
I looked for my drink, but it went for a swim,
Maybe next time, I'll just order a pin!

A Tropical Reverie Under Stars

With stars like confetti, the sky's in a spark,
The moon's throwing shade, oh, what a lark!
Turtles in tuxes chat 'neath the glow,
While I trip on a flip-flop, just stealing the show!

This night is a giggle, sweet tunes fill the air,
While crickets audition for leading roles rare.
A firefly's solo illuminates my plight,
As I dance with a crab, not a soul in sight.

Journey Through Aquamarine Dreams

In waters like jelly, I float without care,
Fish in bright suits swim, oh what a flair!
I wave to a sea star, it gives me a wink,
While a clam on a date snaps—what do you think?

An octopus juggles some shells and a shell,
I'm laughing so hard, it's hard to quell.
As jellyfish giggle in frolicsome grace,
I tumble back home, still stuck in this race.

Hues of Paradise in Motion

Under the sun, a dance begins,
Fish in tuxedos, wearing grins.
Coral reefs laugh, bursting with flair,
Crabs doing conga, we stop and stare.

A parrotfish sings with a voice so bright,
While sea turtles glide, soaring in flight.
Jellyfish jive, in a sassy display,
Even the clams join the show, hey hey!

Caress of the Warm Ebb

Waves tickle toes in a playful tease,
Seashells gossip with the rustling breeze.
Sandcastles crumble, their reign is brief,
Still, they wave goodbye like a king in relief.

Starfish throw parties, no need for a shell,
With sea cucumbers, they mix and dwell.
Laughter erupts from a distant buoy,
As seagulls play catch, all filled with joy!

Mysteries of the Shimmering Depths

Fishes in fancy hats sneak a peek,
While clams tell jokes, it's a funny streak.
A seaweed monster curls up in glee,
"Don't mind me, just playing hide and sea!"

Octopuses mimic, their skills on show,
Dancing in rhythm—oh, what a flow!
Tropical bubbles burst out a laugh,
With every float, they chart their own path.

Floating on Celestial Tides

Buoyant dreams drift in a wobbly line,
Starfish play poker, their bets divine.
Dolphins leap high, with a splashy cheer,
Who knew the sea held such comedy here!

Mermaids giggle, their hair all a-froth,
"Who needs a mirror when we have a cloth?"
Anemones wiggle, tickling the breeze,
As fish share secrets, aiming to please.

Vows of Mermaids and Sailors

In a cove, where mermaids sing,
Sailors swear to wear a bling.
They toss their nets and dive for crabs,
While laughing hard, they lose their jabs.

The mermaids giggle, take a bubble bath,
Sailors try to dance, but feel the wrath.
One mermaid winks, with a cheeky grin,
As the sailor slips and takes a spin.

With nets and shells, they trade their tales,
Sailors trade anchors, mermaids trade scales.
Each rival claims the best of seas,
But both get stuck in seaweed trees.

They vow to meet with drinks in hand,
While plotting tricks upon the sand.
But when the tide rolls in at night,
Both end up waving, what a sight!

The Pulse of Island Life

On a sunny day, with feckless glee,
Seagulls squawk, and kids race free.
A piña colada spills on the floor,
As sunbathers wake up from the snore.

The beach ball bounces, a dog gives chase,
Grannies chase kids, it's a comical race.
A coconut falls, they all duck down,
Laughter erupts; it's the best clown town!

Fish flip-flop in a grill debate,
Who's the best catch? It's a funny fate.
Yet all agree on late-night fries,
With sandy toes beneath starlit skies.

So gather the tribe; bring your own flare,
Dance in the sand without a care.
Island life pulses a jovial tune,
Under the loving light of the moon.

Chasing Shadows on the Beach

A sunbeam darts like a daring cat,
Chasing shadows, imagine that!
Kids run fast with sand in shoes,
Throwing laughter, mixing blues.

Hopscotch lines with seashell marks,
While crabs hold court, acting stark.
A kite gets stuck in a palm tree's hold,
As everyone laughs, it's pure gold.

Flip-flops flying, what a sight!
Totally hilarious, what pure delight!
Sandcastles crash, they stand and laugh,
It's a goofy, sandy epitaph.

In golden light, they frolic and play,
With silly tricks planned for the day.
Shadows race till the sun bids goodbye,
As giggles linger 'neath the twilight sky.

Sonnet of the Rolling Surf

The waves crash in with a playful cheer,
Surfboards tumble like they've lost their rear.
A beach bum waves, with sunscreen smeared,
    Squeals of joy, it's greeting feared!

    With every roll, the surf does tease,
As folks try to stand, they slip with ease.
A dog barks loud, stealing a snack,
"Hey, that's mine!" is a common quack.

A sailor shouts, "Watch my cool tricks!"
But ends up hugging the ocean's bricks.
Laughter erupts as they splash and play,
    Under the sun, it's a legendary day.

In salty air, funny tales are spun,
As shades of summer blend and run.
Rolling surf, with giggles it conveys,
The silliest of joy in sun-kissed rays.

Canvas of Coral and Fantasy

A fish with a hat, oh what a sight!
He dances with crab, under moonlight.
They sip on punch made of seaweed swirl,
While jellyfish twirl in a sapphire whirl.

The sea turtle smiles, doing the cha-cha,
With a rhythm that's wavy from here to afar.
A dolphin brings snacks, all shaped like stars,
As octopuses juggle, applause from the bars.

Clams sing in harmony, quite off-key,
While seahorses gossip about their new spree.
Lobsters on trumpets, what a weird band,
A lively soirée in a seaweed strand.

Sandcastles rise like towers of gold,
With snails in the tower, ambitions unfold.
A crab in a tux, with a top hat so bright,
Says, "Join my ball – it's a wild, silly night!"

Sanctuary of the Sea Spirits

In a cove where seahorses sip on mint tea,
Mermaids compete in the great giggle spree.
With shells as their trophies, they laugh and they dance,
As starfish play maracas in a bizarre trance.

The lighthouse is blushing, wearing a wig,
While clams crack jokes, each one quite big.
Manatees giggle, their bubbles take flight,
Joining in on the fun, giggles echo through night.

Pirates of laughter, treasure of glee,
Trade stories with shrimp, sipping saltwater tea.
An octopus DJ spins tunes with delight,
While turtles in shades glide under moonlight.

In this haven of chuckles, the crabs take their place,
With rhinestone shells flaunting a cool, stylish grace.
Bubbles burst into laughter, a splashy encore,
This sanctuary's quirky, who could want more?

Marooned in Blissful Solitude

A castaway crab found a coconut hat,
He claimed it his throne, 'I'm royalty, that!'
Beneath swaying palms, he practices his wave,
But seagulls just chuckle, "Oh, what a knave!"

With a parrot on shoulder, they plot a great feast,
But the fruits keep on rolling, their fun's never ceased.
A pig in a snorkel took a dip in the bay,
Declaring, "I'm free! Who needs to go play?"

Coconuts laugh as they tumble and roll,
The crab with his crown feels quite in control.
But berries get jealous, roll right off the tree,
"Hey, come have a party, you're stuck here with me!"

Is it a simple life, living beachside aloof?
Or a carnival chaos, with not much to prove?
The sand whispers softly, "Just go with the flow,"
As laughter ignites like a breezy tableau.

Petals in the Wind and Water

Daisies float by, on waves of a song,
They swish and they sway, where nothing feels wrong.
A butterfly thinks it should waltz with a fish,
With a splash and a twirl, they fulfill every wish.

The breeze carries tales of a playful sea frog,
Who hops on the currents, a vibrant sea smog.
While bubbles rise high, they pop like balloons,
Encouraging crabs to dance under the dunes.

Water lilies gossip under sunny beams bright,
Sharing secrets of love that glimmer at night.
While pufferfish puff, adding colors and flair,
Playing hot potato with a splashy ol' chair.

Floating on petals, lost in this mirth,
With fish wearing ties, planning fun at the hearth.
A great big sea party where giggles don't cease,
In this whimsical world, they're all dancing in peace!

Resonance of Whispering Waves

Tiny crabs in a race, oh what a sight,
Their tiny legs scuttle with all their might.
Seashells gossip, they chatter away,
While a starfish plays peekaboo with the bay.

A dolphin with shades takes a splash,
While seagulls compete in a fishy bash.
Sandcastles jealous of towers so grand,
Waves come crashing, they can't understand.

Jellyfish dance like they're at a ball,
With each flip and flop, they're having a ball.
Crabs in tuxedos go waltzing by,
With conch shells echoing a soft, sweet sigh.

When the sun sets low, and colors blend,
They plot their escape, the sea is their friend.
With laughter and splashes, oh what a tease,
Let's all join in on this jolly freeze!

Stars in the Caribbean Sky

Beneath a blanket of shimmering light,
Stars giggle, twinkling with pure delight.
A moon with a grin gives a wink and a nudge,
While coconuts swing, they just won't budge.

Tropical fish, all dressed in bright hues,
Practice their lines, rehearsing their cues.
Mermaids with mirrors, they're combing their hair,
While a lazy turtle just doesn't care.

Chasing the breeze, a kite takes a dive,
Declaring, 'I'm king, watch me thrive!'
Clouds join the fun, in a fluffy parade,
As laughter erupts from the sea's masquerade.

Stars trade their secrets, oh what a show,
As the wave whispers softly, 'Come on, let's go!'
The night's filled with chuckles, shimmer on sand,
In this Caribbean dream, all is well planned!

Tides of Hope and Adventure

With a bucket and spade, the pirates set sail,
For seas full of treasures, they'll never fail.
But instead of gold, they find only shoes,
And old jellybeans, with funny blues clues.

Crabs in a parade, a snappy delight,
Marching along, what a curious sight!
A parrot named Gemma sings tunes that astound,
While the waves gently giggle, a bubbly sound.

A fish dons a hat, quite dapper and neat,
With a tuba in fins, he keeps quite the beat.
Mermaids join in, splashing sparks in the air,
Creating a symphony, beyond compare!

Adventure awaits just beyond the shore,
With each silly twist, we always want more.
Under the sun, with laughter so grand,
The tides of our dreams make a whimsical land!

Ballad of the Mango Breeze

In the shade of a mango, oh what a thrill,
A monkey named Louie is making a spill.
With nectar so sweet, on a hot summer's day,
He swings from the branches, then zooms away!

Kites flying high, with stripes like a clown,
Dance with a rhythm, oh look at them go down!
They tangle in laughter, they giggle and play,
Playing tag with the wind that won't go away.

The breeze carries whispers of fruits on a spree,
While crickets provide the late-night symphony.
Fireflies twinkle like jolly old stars,
While the moon takes a selfie with its night-time cars.

Mangoes are rolling, a festival bright,
With laughter and joy, our spirits take flight.
In this tropical dance, we twirl 'round with ease,
Our hearts full of sunshine, in the mango breeze!

Threads of Sunlight and Water

In a floaty, rickety boat,
I tried to catch a fish with a coat,
The fish just laughed, took a leap,
As I splashed and fell in, oh so deep!

Seagulls giggled, in skies so blue,
They squawked, "Nice swim, we'll leave it to you!"
With sun-kissed waves and sand on my nose,
I swam with bubbles, what fun it bestows!

In the Embrace of Salt and Sky

With a coconut hat, I danced on the shore,
My friends laughed hard, they couldn't want more,
The tide stole my flip-flops, oh what a steal,
Now I'm barefoot, but that's part of the deal!

Seashells chimed in, a concert most grand,
As I juggled beach balls that slipped from my hand,
The sun set low, like a lazy old cat,
We all took a picture with a crab on my hat!

Murmurs from the Waves' Heart

The waves whispered secrets, oh what could they mean?
Perhaps they were plotting a sandy routine,
With a quick little splash, they tickled my toes,
I fell in the surf, much to my woes!

A clam threw a party, I thought it was great,
But the guest list was seaweed, I had to vacate,
With a wink and a wave, I bid them adieu,
"Next time, dear friends, I'll bring snacks for you!"

Journeys to the Dreamy Isles

On a rafts of floaties, we sailed with delight,
But drifted so far, we lost sight of the light,
With snacks and giggles, we cried out for land,
But the only response was the sea's busy hand!

We found an isle, it turned out to be,
A pile of coconuts, not quite our spree,
We built a tall tower, but it fell with a thud,
Now we're all stuck, just a bunch of nutty buds!

Banquet of Seashells and Stars

In a shell, a crab wore a crown,
He declared himself king of the town.
The guests were clams, dancing with glee,
While seagulls squawked, "Join the jam, let's see!"

With jellyfish jello and seaweed stew,
The fish was a chef, all decked out in blue.
They served up the laughs on plates made of sand,
While dolphins juggled seashells—oh, wasn't it grand!

A starfish in boots pranced around so spry,
While a turtle made rhymes that made the crabs cry.
The waves clapped their hands with a splashy cheer,
As the party rolled on, full of joy, never fear!

As the moonlit tide tucked them into their beds,
The starfish whispered secrets with wiggly threads.
"Tomorrow," he said, with a wink in his eye,
"Let's hold a parade where the seaweed can fly!"

Whims of Nature on Paradise Shore

On a beach where the coconuts danced in delight,
A crab tried on sunglasses, oh what a sight!
He strutted and shuffled, a true fashionista,
While the fish in the tide sang like a diva!

Seagulls wore hats, all tilted and cool,
While the waves played tag—what a mischievous pool!
A clam with a ukulele strummed out a tune,
As the sun set its stage, lighting up the dunes.

An octopus juggled colorful shells,
Telling tales of the deep where the laughter dwells.
The breeze blew confetti, made from the foam,
While the sand tickled toes, calling them home.

When twilight arrived, with giggles and glee,
The hermit crabs lined up for a comedy spree.
In paradise moments, nature unveiled,
That whimsy and wonder will never be jailed!

The Silence of Retreating Waves

When the waves pull back, they giggle and sigh,
"Let's play peek-a-boo!" they whisper and cry.
The sand dollars chuckle, rolling around,
While clams hold their breath, barely making a sound.

In the shallows, a fish tries to dance on a shell,
But slips on a starfish, oh what a fell!
The sea foam is laughing, all bubbly and sly,
As the tide swirls and twirls, a watery high.

Beneath the blue, where the turtles get lost,
They race with the current, whatever the cost.
A crab with a walk that's more wobble than stride,
Cried out, "Who's the best? Come and take me for a ride!"

As the water retreats, stories ripple away,
But they know they'll return at the break of the day.
So let's laugh at the ebb and dance with the flow,
For in the depths of the sea, there's always a show!

Mirage of the Island Heart

A coconut gently fell with a thud,
I thought it was treasure, but it was just mud.
Dancing with crabs under the bright sun,
They've got the moves, I can't seem to run.

Palm trees are swaying, feeling quite bold,
Their shadows like stories waiting to be told.
I slip on a shell, oh what a sight,
The crabs laugh aloud, they're having a night!

Wave after wave, they splash all around,
A fish with a hat is the talk of the town.
He winks with a grin, thinks he's a big shot,
But I see his fins; he's got quite a lot!

On this sandy stage, I find my delight,
With giggles and waves guiding my flight.
The beauty is silly, the silliness true,
An island so wild, it's taunting me too!

The Colors of Salty Serenades

A parrot croons tunes with a beak made of gold,
While fish in a line play a fairy tale told.
They flash their bright scales, like jewels in the sun,
Yet all I can think is, how can we have fun?

Mermaids are giggling, they've started a chase,
They gave me a wave, I just fell on my face.
Their laughter is sweet, echoing through the breeze,
I wave back in style, hoping to please.

The sand's like a blanket, so cozy and warm,
Except when you stand, and it gives your feet harm.
I juggle some seashells, I think I'm a star,
But one falls and rolls; it's gone, oh so far!

As sunset comes dancing, the sky gets aglow,
The giggles and colors put on quite a show.
With pals by my side and laughter so bright,
Life feels just right, under stars in the night!

Harmony of the Coral Reefs

In the underwater world, fish play band,
With a jellyfish drummer, oh isn't it grand?
They jive with the currents, looking so proud,
While I watch from above, feeling lost in the crowd.

A sea cucumber winks, says, "Come join the spree!"
But I fumble and trip on a bemused little bee.
It chuckles and rolls, as I'm caught in a splash,
Making memories that came in a flash.

The seaweed is dancing to each happy note,
While starfish compose songs in a curious coat.
I join in their rhythm, feeling so slick,
But one big wave says, "Oops! Better stick!"

Harmony thrives in this aquatic ballet,
A comical ensemble that brightens my day.
Each twirl and each flip is a joyous parade,
In the depths of the reef, where good vibes are laid!

Breezy Promises at Sundown

The sunset spills colors like ice cream delight,
A cat that just stole my last beachside bite.
It struts with such flair, like a king on his throne,
While I watch in despair, as my snack is all gone!

Waves are gossiping softly, sharing fun tales,
Of turtles with sunglasses, and windsurfing snails.
They've got the cool moves, riding the swell,
While I trip on my flip-flops and tumble as well.

The seagulls all giggle, calling their friends,
"Look at that human, where does this end?"
I join in their laughter, my face in the sand,
While grains tickle my nose, it's a wild, crazy land!

The day drifts to close, with fireflies in flight,
As promises shimmer in the fading light.
With each laugh and mishap, I savor it still,
For life by the shore is a blissful goodwill!

Luminous Echoes of Nature's Heart

Under the sun, a crab does dance,
Strutting sideways without a chance.
Fish wear sunglasses, chilling in style,
While seaweed giggles all the while.

Bubbles rise up, they seem to chatter,
A starfish claims it's worth a platter.
Seagulls caw jokes from way up high,
While dolphins dive with a gleeful sigh.

Octopuses juggle, it's quite a show,
While clams play cards, oh what a row!
The tide rolls in like a playful pup,
As sandcastles crumble, the sea says "sup!"

Everyone's laughing, so carefree and bright,
With shells as hats, they party all night.
In this quirky world, where joy can be found,
Nature's heart beats with laughter all around.

Brewed in the Latte of the Sea

Each wave whispers tales, a caffeinated brew,
A mermaid spills coffee, it's quite the view.
Sea turtles sip lattes, foam on their shells,
While jellyfish serve donuts, oh who could tell?

Sandy baristas, with shells for their bows,
Whip up frothy drinks with seaweed flows.
Sea cucumbers wiggle in pretty berets,
As they serve up laughter in curious ways.

The seafoam froths like a milkshake delight,
While crabs share secrets in the soft twilight.
With coconut cups and anemone straws,
The flavors of laughter fill the ocean's jaws.

So raise your glass to the waves' merry cheer,
A beachside café that's never austere.
With every splash, the fun's sure to please,
Luxury sips, brewed in the latte of the seas.

Melodies of Beneath the Waves

Fish play flutes made of coral and sand,
While seahorses dance in a synchronized band.
Bubble notes rise, in a splashy refrain,
Singing with crabs in a whimsical train.

Turtles tap dance on soft seaweed floors,
While whales compose with deep, booming roars.
Clams keep the beat with a rhythmic clap,
As squids paint the music with every flap.

The sea's a concert, oh what a delight,
As conch shells echo into the night.
Under the waves, a symphony brews,
With laughter and joy in melodious hues.

So swim on down for a front-row seat,
To the melodies flow, oh what a treat!
In the dance of the tides, let your spirit soar,
As nature's orchestra plays evermore.

The Palette of the Sun-Kissed Waters

Splash of pink, a clownfish on the drift,
While starfish dazzle, a colorful gift.
Corals brush laughter in wavy strokes,
Brightening smiles with their quirky jokes.

The ocean's a canvas, splattered with fun,
Where sea turtles paint under the sun.
Shrimp in tutus twirl with delight,
As colors collide in a joyous light.

With a splash of humor and a wink of a tail,
Dolphins dive in, they never go pale.
Each ripple reflects a rainbow so bold,
While clam shells giggle, their stories are told.

So dance with the tide, embrace every hue,
In this wacky world, there's plenty to do.
The palette of laughter begins with the seas,
Where nature creates a masterpiece with ease.

Journey to the Shimmering Beyond.

We danced with crabs on sandy shores,
While seagulls plotted mischief galore.
A flip-flop flew, it made a great splat,
Who knew beach days could be like that?

With sunscreen fights and laughter so loud,
We built a sandcastle, oh so proud.
But guard it well, for waves like to sneak,
And turn your fortress into a creek!

The puffer fish joined our silly parade,
Wobbling and bobbling, oh what a charade!
A pair of dolphins burst into song,
While we tossed coconuts all day long.

So here's to the splashes, the sun, and the snacks,
With flip-flops flying as we dodged the attacks.
In this land of giggles, we all fit right in,
In a crazy tropical world, let the fun begin!

Whispers of the Tidal Night

The stars above twinkle with delight,
As crabs decide to dance through the night.
They've got moves that could make anyone cheer,
But watch your toes, they're not really clear!

The jellyfish glows like a disco ball,
At the midnight beach, we're having a ball.
With beachball bombs and a splashy fight,
We're the silliest crew under the moonlight.

A parrot squawks jokes in a hilarious tone,
While fish giggle softly, not wanting to groan.
With waves that bubble in playful arcs,
We laugh until our faces leave marks.

So come, my friends, let's eat some treats,
With sand in our hair, and sticky sweet beats.
As whispers of tides cradle us tight,
We merge with the laughter of this funny night.

Serenade of the Coral Reefs

Corals hum softly a tune so bright,
While clownfish are laughing at their own sight.
With seaweed wigs and a dolphin DJ,
They host underwater parties all day!

Octopus twirls in a polka dot dress,
While the starfish juggles, oh what a mess!
We joined the conch shells flinging out beats,
With sea turtles busting some fancy feats.

The sea cucumber said, "Let's have a ball,"
But with no legs, it just took a crawl.
And that's when the sharks burst in with a grin,
"Let's dance, dear friends, and celebrate fin!"

In this reef full of giggles and rays,
We spun in the currents, lost track of days.
In the warmth of the waters, we share our cheer,
With the quirky cast of the underwater sphere.

Beneath a Tropical Moon

Beneath the moon, a coconut fell,
Bouncing off heads – oh, what a swell!
We cracked it open by sheer accident,
And laughter erupted, such time well spent!

The geckos took charge, leading the game,
As we tried to catch them, all just the same.
Flip-flops abandoned on our wild chase,
As we tangled in vines, what a hilarious race!

With fireflies shining like lights on our crew,
We serenaded the night with a raucous woohoo!
The glow of the sand made it all so bright,
As hiccups from laughter echoed in night.

So here's to the fun, the zany and bold,
Underneath the moon, as the stories unfold.
With food fights and splashes, we'll always recall,
Our wild tropical nights where we laughed through it all!

Jaded Horizons and Golden Sands

Seagulls arguing over fries,
Crabs in tiny costumes, oh my!
Sunburned tourists doing the dance,
While waves crash in a merry trance.

A beach ball stuck in a tree,
Pineapples wearing shades, can't you see?
Shells whisper secrets to the breeze,
As flip-flops throw a fashion tease.

Sandcastles teeter, a royal mess,
With moats so shallow, we must confess,
The tide laughs hard at our grand plan,
As we sip drinks from a strange tan can.

But under palm trees, joy's in command,
We stumble forth on a golden strand.
In this silly paradise, we take our stand,
With laughter echoing, life is unplanned.

The Scent of Ocean-Salted Kisses

The breeze smells like sunscreen and dreams,
Fish in sunglasses strike silly schemes.
Turtles zoom past in a race so grand,
While dolphins giggle at our band.

A crab in a hat is running for mayor,
While seaweed whispers, "Aren't we in despair?"
Splashing waves have their own gossip,
As our beach games go all topsy-turvy tip!

Chasing seagulls with popcorn galore,
They squawk a protest, "We want more!"
Under the sun with sparkle and cheer,
Eating ice cream with a side of smears.

For each splash tells a tale, every wave a jest,
In this salty realm, we're truly blessed.
With giggles and sunshine, we jest and play,
In our funny beach world, let's laugh the day away.

Clarity Found in Turquoise Depths

Snorkels on, we dive and we sway,
Fish swim by, stealing the buffet.
Lost goggles make a fashion statement,
While flippers start a dance tournament.

Sea urchins grinning, what a sight!
They throw a party under the moonlight.
While starfish try to cha-cha and spin,
We're left wondering where to begin.

Mermaids blow bubbles, making us laugh,
As conch shells grace the autograph.
With a dolphin duo cracking jokes,
We clap and cheer, our minds it provokes!

For clarity shines as we flounder about,
In this watery fun, we jump and we shout.
The turquoise depths hold secrets to chase,
In bubbles of joy, we find our place.

Serenities Stitched by Gentle Breezes

A hammock swings, what a dreamy life,
As ants hold fashion shows, rife with strife.
Coconuts roll, their laughter so sweet,
While geckos eye us with quick little feet.

The sun sneezes, and we shield our eyes,
Shells recite tales beneath the skies.
With every gust, a giggle's born,
As we navigate this sandy corn.

Funny hats float, swimmingly thick,
The wind's a comedian; oh, what a trick!
We laugh as we chase a kite in the air,
While the waves wink, without a care.

So here we sway with a rhythm so nice,
In playful echoes, life's funny slice.
With whispers of breezes, we find our bliss,
In stitches of laughter, we can't help but kiss.

Cascade of Sun and Sea

Waves giggle softly on the beach,
Sea foam tickles toes within reach.
A crab in a tuxedo struts by,
While seagulls steal fries with a sly eye.

Lifeguards in shades, they're posing strong,
But trip on their boards and they can't be wrong.
Sandcastles crumble with laughter in tow,
As beach balls bounce like they own the show.

Tanned folks debate on who's the best tan,
While dolphins perform like they're in a band.
The sun's a comedian, shining bright,
As flip-flops fly into the tropical night.

Heartbeats Beneath the Palm Trees

Palm trees sway with a rhythm unclear,
While tourists stumble, spilling their beer.
The breeze tells jokes as it whistles by,
And coconut cups wobble, oh my, oh my!

Beneath the shade, lovers proclaim,
That "this is the spot," yet they forget their name.
With sand in their toes and salt in their hair,
Each heartbeat's a dance, a whimsical flair.

A crab silently judges, its eyes open wide,
As beachgoers argue over the tide.
The waves roll in with a laughter so grand,
While sunburned tourists can't quite understand.

Marigold Sunsets and Celestial Dreams

Sunsets spill colors like spilled paint,
While a seagull on a tree threatens to faint.
The sky wears a grin, all orange and gold,
As beach blankets rustle, just a bit bold.

Flip-flops are flying like they've lost control,
As kids dig for treasure, each one a patrol.
The sun bows low, puts on a shy show,
While surfers ride waves that swirl down below.

In the distance, a ukulele strums,
As a cat on a surfboard sings about crumbs.
Marigold skies with starlight to beam,
All while we giggle and chase our own dream.

The Enchantment of Hidden Coves

In hidden coves where secrets hide,
A fish in sunglasses takes a wild ride.
Turtles move slow, pretending to race,
While mermaids giggle, escaping the chase.

The tide rolls in with a splash and a pop,
As snorkelers bumble, like bubbles they drop.
Each stone tells a tale, all funny and bright,
Of whispers and chuckles passed through the night.

Clams crack jokes with their shells all ajar,
While sailors debate if they've gone too far.
In this quirky cove, life spins like a dream,
As laughter and waves weave the brightest theme.

Coral Cradle at Dusk

Bubbles rise to greet the sun,
Fishes giggle, having fun.
Seashells cheer, they clap and sway,
Dancing crabs all join the play.

Tropical breeze, a ticklish tick,
Starfish laugh, oh what a trick!
Jellyfish waltz with jelly beans,
While dolphins plot their silly schemes.

Flip-flops flop on sandy shore,
Each wave a joke, they can't ignore.
Gull's squawking, "What's the deal?"
Mermaids blush, "We can't conceal!"

As twilight paints the sky's big canvas,
Turtles tease, "Who's got the madness?"
With one last splash, the day does fade,
Under pink skies, the fun parade!

Driftwood Lullabies

Driftwood sings a silly tune,
Crabs tap dance beneath the moon.
Sea turtles snore while sharks have dreams,
Of flashy fins and pudding creams.

Waves roll in with belly laughs,
Clowns of fish, all drawn with gaffes.
Oysters wink with every wave,
Pearls of laughter, oh how they crave!

A starfish juggles bits of kelp,
Finding treasures, zig and yelp.
Seagulls swirl with flapping glee,
Telling tales of fish they see.

In sunset's glow, the water shines,
Driftwood hums its playful lines.
As dreams take flight on tides of glee,
Silly whispers float, wild and free!

Swaying Palms and Stardust

Palms do the limbo, swaying nice,
While coconuts roll like a dice.
Parrots squawk a raucous cheer,
As crabs throw shells, "Come join us here!"

Frisky breeze tickles the sand,
Footprints lead to a party planned.
Flip-flops flop on bamboo tunes,
Dancing shadows under moons.

Kites fly high like pirate ships,
As jellybeans bounce, do flips.
Colorful fish wear hats of style,
Making every splash worthwhile.

The sun dips low in a peachy hue,
With starry winks and skies so blue.
Cuddly critters sing and sway,
As night draws near, they laugh and play.

Moonlit Waters and Heartbeats

Moonbeams twinkle, water's gleam,
Fiddler crabs with joyful schemes.
Starlight whispers, "What's the catch?"
As seahorses make a daring match.

Waves tickle toes in a silly fight,
Splashing seagulls take to flight.
Dancing snails upon the shore,
Leave trails of giggles, that's for sure!

Pirate parrots squawk in rhyme,
"Let's sail the tide, it's fun time!"
With treasures from the sandy floor,
They giggle loud, and then explore.

In moonlit laughter, joy expands,
As fishy pals give high five hands.
Hearts beat fast in this playful night,
As dreams sail on, the stars ignite!

Luminescent Shores at Dusk

Twinkling sands beneath our feet,
Crafting castles that can't compete.
A crab with swagger, he takes a stroll,
Waving his claws like he's on patrol.

Shells hold secrets, or so they say,
But mostly just beach snacks that went astray.
A seagull swoops, aiming for fries,
Then flies off, leaving us in surprise.

Flip-flops fling with every stride,
As we bounce to the sound of the tide.
Sunset paint, the sky a prank,
Turning our smiles into a loud clank.

Salty air, it tickles the nose,
While someone trips—oh, there it goes!
Laughter erupts, like bubbles in soft
With memories that rise and lift us aloft.

The Rhythm of Tidal Echoes

Waves go whoosh, they tease our toes,
Drawing back like a playful nose.
A dolphin jumps, but slips on foam,
Making us laugh from our beach-side dome.

The tide hums tunes, a giggling breeze,
It dances past, aiming to please.
A starfish tries to steal the spotlight,
But gets flipped over, what a funny sight!

Children chase the sea with glee,
While tides chase kids, what a spree!
A hermit crab wears someone's shell,
"Look at me!" it shouts, "A fashion bell!"

Sandcastles crumble with a loud crash,
Leaving behind just a sandy splash.
Too many tales, all funny and bold,
In waves that dance, in stories told.

Reflections in the Azure Depths

Splashing through the bright blue sea,
We spotted a fish, then it saw me!
It winked and flipped, a slippery tease,
"Can you catch me?" it laughed on the breeze.

Flip-flops zoomed as we chased its game,
Over sand and rocks, we felt no shame.
Underwater, a clown fish took note,
Making faces, it stole the showboat.

Crabs clapping, practicing their dance,
In a party that needed a chance!
A group of kids laughed all around,
Turning the ocean floor into a sound.

Under the sun, our giggles join,
Like glittering seeds in the salty coin.
Our laughter floats, like bubbles that roam,
Always together, the seaside feels like home.

Salty Kisses of the Trade Winds

The breeze arrives with a cheeky kiss,
Wiggling my hair, what a funny bliss!
It tickles my face, makes me giggle wide,
As I chase after waves like a joyful ride.

A parrot squawks, "You're too slow, friend!"
While I stumble over beach gear to mend.
Peanut butter sandwiches flying away,
Thanks to the winds' mischievous play!

Sunsets play tricks with shadows that dance,
Twisting and turning, they take a chance.
In a wobbly boat, we set up for fun,
But who knew it'd flip like a toasted bun?

As palm trees sway, we strut our stuff,
Laughing at life through each little puff.
The trade winds blow, with humor and grace,
Filling our hearts, we embrace this space.

Cascading Lights of the Moonlit Bay

Bubbles rise and fish can dance,
A crab in shorts took a chance.
The moon spills gold on silly waves,
As dolphins dive like merry knaves.

Starfish play a game of tag,
While mermaids giggle, quite the brag.
They sip on coconut, oh so sweet,
And dance to rhythms with their feet.

A seagull squawks like it's on stage,
While turtles shuffle, they're quite sage.
The night is wild, no time for fears,
We toast with shells and laugh in cheers.

So come and join this beach-side feast,
Where laughter flows, not just the yeast.
The bay will sparkle, a joyful view,
Where silly dreams become so true.

An Odyssey of Sandy Escapes

Sandcastles crumble, what a plight,
As seagulls swoop, it's quite the sight.
A beach ball bounces, nearly hits me,
Chasing it down feels like a spree.

Sunburned noses and slushies in hand,
The tide pulls back, a sneaky strand.
We dive for treasures, shells shiny bright,
Counting the crabs, quite the delight.

Flip-flops flying, oh what a show!
As clumsy kids go with the flow.
Fins in the water, laughter erupts,
Splashing around, oh how we jump!

Sandy escapes on this funny ride,
With giggles echoing, we start to glide.
Each wave brings jokes, of sun and spray,
Creating memories that happily stay.

The Tale Weaved by the Tides

A fish in a hat, now that's a sight,
Dancing with crabs under the moonlight.
They spin around in merry glee,
While jellyfish join, oh what a spree!

The stars start to play hide and seek,
As sea turtles twirl, so unique.
A conch shell whispers tales of old,
Of treasure maps and pirates bold.

But here on the shore, our laughter swells,
With silly stories that no one tells.
The tide returns with splashes bright,
Mixing our dreams with the cool night.

We laugh and boast of careful feats,
As flip-flops fly and the ocean greets.
Each wave brings joy, and tales unwind,
Under the moon, we're all entwined.

Infinity Beneath the Aqua Sky

Under the sun, what a wild ride,
Flipping with waves as they rush and glide.
Pelicans dive for a fishy snack,
While sandy toes try to run back.

A pirate's hat on a dolphin's head,
Makes everyone giggle, with joy widespread.
They sing of treasures and chests of gold,
While the seafloor chuckles, its secrets told.

Laughter and splashes, what a display,
As kids in the water giggle and play.
With sunbeams dancing on our warm skin,
We chase our dreams, let the fun begin!

So join in the chaos that's fun and free,
Beneath the vast sky, as bright as can be.
The giggles and splashes, oh what a sight,
In this world of wonder, we take flight!

Treasure Maps in the Sand

On the beach, drawing squiggly lines,
Hoping to find gold among the pines.
But it's just a flip-flop, a stray sock,
Guess my treasure's a pair of crocs!

With each wave, my map will change,
As sea gulls cackle, 'Ain't that strange?'
I dug a hole, with dreams so grand,
Only to find a lost dog's band!

X marks the spot where my plan went wrong,
Little crabs join in, singing a song.
A pot of gold? Try rubber ducks,
It seems my fortune really sucks!

So I'll laugh and sip my coconut drink,
While pirates roll over in sandy stink.
Adventure waits on this sandy shore,
With laughter, who really needs more?

Hummingbirds at Dawn's First Light

Flitting about, with speed and grace,
Sipping nectar, a silly race.
Wings a blur, like a buzzing bee,
"Hey, that's my flower!" said the bee.

Morning comes and they start to chime,
Chasing each other, oh what a crime!
"You're too slow!" one little bird teases,
While another gets stuck, lost in the breezes.

With colors so bright, they put on a show,
The sun's up now, time to go, go, go!
They zip past the piña colada stand,
And laugh at a crab with a drink in hand.

While the world wakes up to their sweet ballet,
I sip my coffee and shout, "Hooray!"
For all the joy these small ones bring,
While a pelican drops in, just to sing.

Dances of the Swelling Foam

The waves twirl 'round like a wacky dance,
Flipping and flopping, a wobbly prance.
With foam hats bobbing on top of each crest,
They seem to say, "Come join our fest!"

Seashells applaud with a clinky sound,
As sea turtles move to the beat they've found.
A starfish hops, though it's not quite right,
"Dance like a crab, but hold on tight!"

The dolphins dive in with splashes of cheer,
While a fishy chorus shouts, "We're all here!"
A mackerel slips, trips, and goes flop,
Leaving all of us in a laughing nonstop.

So under the sun, we join in the fun,
With sandy feet, we get it done.
Next time you're near where the waters churn,
Watch for the party, it's your turn!

Soliloquy of the Rolling Swell

Oh, mighty swell, you think you're grand,
Rolling in waves, like you own the land.
But I'll tell you, my dear bubbling friend,
You sometimes spill dreams, right to the end!

With each rise and fall, such poetic flair,
You toss my beach ball, without a care.
And I chase after, with laughter and fright,
While you bubble along, sipping moonlight.

"Hey, get back here!" I holler in play,
As you tease my toes, then splash away.
You flip my plans like a grand marionette,
"Who needs a map?" I ask with a threat.

So here's to you, the slippery tide,
With your silly dance, I take it in stride.
For life's too short, let's just splash and swell,
As long as you promise to not break the shell!

Ripples of Forgotten Dreams

The fish wear hats, they dance with glee,
While crabs tap toes and sing off-key.
Seashells gossip about their day,
As seagulls cackle, "Hey, come play!"

Palm trees sway to the coconut beat,
A dolphin slides on a slippery seat.
Sunshine giggles, the waves all cheer,
As flip-flops vanish, oh dear, oh dear!

Sandcastles rise, then tumble down,
With moats of water that wear a frown.
Starfish wear socks, and clams like to dance,
In this twisted, nautical, silly romance!

So grab your floaties, don your shades,
Let's wade through these whimsical glades.
We'll swirl and twirl, give a splash and a shout,
In this silly world, with laughter throughout!

A Sailor's Reverie

A sailor dreams of fish in ties,
Who hold board meetings under bright blue skies.
Their debates on seaweed, now that's a dish!
While turtles serve tea; Oh, what a wish!

His ship's a banana, floating free,
With sails of candy, yes, you see!
They race with crabs; it's quite absurd,
With seagulls shouting, "Now that's the word!"

The compass spins like aoyoyo jest,
To find a treasure—a crab in a vest!
They laugh and hoot in salty cheer,
As their laughter echoes from ear to ear.

Tales of mishaps fill the ocean air,
Like how jellyfish learned to do a hair.
So hoist the sails for an epic ride,
Through this zany sea, where joys collide!

Flavors of Paradise

Pineapple hats on tropical trees,
With mango smoothies that giggle with ease.
Coconuts play games in the sun,
While limes toss confetti, oh, what fun!

Bananas sing harmony in a band,
As papayas throw parties on the sand.
Watermelons do a salsa twist,
As passion fruit shouts, "You can't resist!"

Fish throw a luau, in flip-flop shoes,
While shrimp fry up their dance floor blues.
Every berry blushes, feeling divine,
In this fruity fiesta, just sip on some wine!

So, taste the laughter, sip the delight,
In this fun-filled feast, all day and night.
With flavors popping like bubbles in cheer,
Come join this party, the fun's right here!

Glistening Sands of Memory

The sand dunes giggle with every breeze,
As clams play charades with silly fees.
Footsteps dance, but flip-flops play hide,
While shells exchange tales, side by side.

Seagulls wear spectacles, reading a book,
As dolphins swim by, with a confident look.
Old bottles whisper secrets of the shore,
About mermaids who'd dance and snore!

Tides tickle toes in this coastal play,
With starfish inventing a new game today.
And nighttime brings out a comedy show,
Where all the sea critters trade jokes in a row!

So let's gather 'round for a sandy delight,
With laughter and joy from morning till night.
For every grain holds a giggle or two,
In this wacky, warm place, just for you!

Gentle Waves and Whispered Wishes

The sea sings softly, what a silly tune,
It tickles my toes, like a playful cartoon.
With crabs doing the cha-cha, oh what a sight,
As seabirds practice their aerial flight.

A dolphin dives deep, looking for lost snacks,
While starfish play poker, joking with clacks.
The sand's got a joke, it tickles my nose,
Laughing in waves, as the sunshine glows.

Mermaids gossip, braiding seaweed hair,
While treasure chests snap with a cranky air.
The shells seem to giggle, hiding their pearls,
In a beachside game, swirling with swirls.

A refreshing cocktail, with umbrellas so bright,
Swirling with flavors, oh what a delight!
The sunsets applaud, in colors so grand,
As I sip and I chuckle, framed by the sand.

Caress of the Tropical Current

The waves softly tickle my big silly feet,
As fishes parade, in a friendly retreat.
A conch takes a selfie, what a wild pose,
While seaweed dances, as funny as it grows.

Otters in shades, surf on the tide,
Board shorts and coolers, they take in their ride.
While pelicans chat, with their beaks full of snacks,
Cracking up over jelly, just cutting loose cracks.

The turtles are pondering, sipping their tea,
Deciding on dances, for a tropical spree.
With coconuts laughing, they spill all their juice,
As I roll on the sand, what a jolly ruse!

A coconut race, oh the chaos is grand,
With laughter and splashes, oh how we all stand!
Seashells are shouting, "What a hoot, come quick!"
In the swirl of the tide, where the fun never quits!

Enchanted Isles in the Twilight

The sun winks down, with a mischievous spark,
While turtles play tag, chasing shadows in the dark.
The palm trees giggle, swaying side to side,
As fireflies dance, in the evening's glide.

A sandcastle crumbles, laughing in defeat,
With brick walls falling, the laughter feels sweet.
The moody sea breeze pulls a silly face,
Waging a tickle war with my personal space.

Lobsters throw a party, in hues of red flair,
With dancing sea cucumbers, spinning in air.
The stars pop like popcorn, in a heavenly show,
As we giggle and share, all the joys that we know.

The moon gently whispers, "Keep the fun up high,"
While the water waves back, a gleam in its eye.
As we drift on our dreams, like boats on a theme,
In this funny, wild world, together we gleam.

Sun-Kissed Horizons

The sun beats down, with a comic flair,
As I chase my flip-flops, they're lost in midair!
With seagulls involved in a jesting parade,
And palm trees flailing, throwing shade while they wave.

The beach ball escapes, rolling towards a crab,
Who throws up his claws, saying, "Hey, don't grab!"
While kids in the sand make castles so tall,
With moats full of giggles, they invite us all.

A picnic unfolds, crumbs scatter like dreams,
While ants join the feast, plotting their schemes.
The sun dips low, painting laughter in gold,
As seashells tell stories, of moments retold.

With bubbles a-flying, we're all in the game,
Laughing together, never feeling the same.
In this silly embrace, as the day bids goodbye,
We dance with the waves, under the twilight sky.

The Dance of the Tropical Breeze

The breeze tickles toes, so light and free,
Palm trees sway, oh what a sight to see!
Laughter bounces with each gust of air,
Who knew a coconut could dance with flair?

A flip-flop army marches down the strand,
With sunburned noses and drinks in hand.
Seagulls squawk their own crazy tune,
While crabs do the cha-cha under the moon!

Every wave a giggle, rolling in shore,
Salty splashes send us squealing for more.
Surfboards wobble like they're on a spree,
When a belly flop means victory!

So raise your glass to this island delight,
Where breezes are mischievous, morning 'til night.
Join the dance, feel the sun's warm tease,
Let's all be silly with the tropical breeze!

Secrets Beneath the Aquamarine

Beneath the waves, where the fish wear hats,
A dolphin tells jokes to sardines and spats.
An octopus juggles, what a sight to behold,
While turtles play poker with cards made of gold.

A clam whispers gossip, so juicy and hot,
While corals perform in a colorful spot.
The sea cucumbers are shy, they don't sing,
But wait till the tide brings out their bling!

Mermaids sip smoothies while swimming in style,
Chatting about the latest sea creature file.
With bubbles of laughter, they swirl and twine,
Trading fishy secrets, oh isn't it fine?

So dive into laughter, don't let the hour fade,
Where silliness thrives in a vibrant parade.
With stories hidden in every marine scene,
Life is a riddle beneath the aquamarine!

Tides of Tomorrow

The tides roll in with a chuckle and tease,
Waves making mischief, as if to please.
A sandcastle's hat flies high in delight,
While the sun plays peek-a-boo, oh what a sight!

Each splash tells a joke, a wave that can laugh,
As seashells giggle, no need for a staff.
Fish in tuxedos swim past with a grin,
While crabs get their groove on, shaking their skin!

The horizon shares tales of tomorrow's fight,
Where clouds puff up like cotton in flight.
As kite-flying birds take a plunge with flair,
The beach turns into a carnival affair!

So let the tides carry your worries away,
With rhythm and mirth, let's jump in and play.
For each twist and turn brings giggles galore,
In the grand ocean show, who could ask for more?

Echoes of the Tropical Horizon

At dawn, the horizon whispers a jest,
As coconuts gather, they're truly the best.
Palm leaves are rustling, oh what do they say?
Maybe it's time for a bright, sunny play!

With sandals in hand, we skip by the shore,
Collecting sweet laughs, oh just one more!
The surf's a comedian, surfboards align,
Wipeouts are treasures, humor divine!

Sunsets dressed in orange, a playful affair,
Cast shadows that dance in the warm, gentle air.
With flip-flops all clapping till stars roam above,
The echoes of laughter and water we love!

So raise your voice high as the horizon beams,
For life's too short, let it burst at the seams.
In every bright moment, we find joy that thrives,
The laughter of tropics, where silliness dives!

www.ingramcontent.com/pod-product-compliance
Lightning Source LLC
Chambersburg PA
CBHW072220070526
44585CB00015B/1417